Parenting Siblings

Guidebook for all parents and families who are expecting new brothers and sisters

Bringing up children as a team, without conflict or jealousy

©2020, Johanna Burgstein

Expertengruppe Verlag

Parenting Siblings

Guidebook for all parents and
families who are expecting new
brothers and sisters

-

Bringing up children as a team,
without conflict or jealousy

Publisher: Expertengruppe Verlag

CONTENTS

ABOUT THE AUTHOR

Johanna Burgstein lives with her husband, Stefan, and her two children Ben (6) and Lena (8) in beautiful Rhineland.

Ever since she studied pedagogy (educational science) more than 10 years ago, she has been addressing subjects related to parenting children. In addition to her main work as a family counsellor, she has been writing an increasing number of papers on these subjects, which is taking up more and more of her time.

In her books, she is particularly interested in subjects where she does not only talk about basic knowledge and theoretical findings, but where she can also share her own experiences. These are not solely experiences from her counselling work, but also include many examples of experiences with her own children.

Every one of her publications, therefore, has its essential scientific basis but is also the result of her own knowledge and experience. With this in mind, she is able to create practical guidebooks, containing a wide range of knowledge and useful tips, which are easy to understand and put into practice.

Johanna Burgstein's easy to read work puts the reader into a relaxed and pleasant ambience, while gaining insight into a subject which most people know something about, but where structure and an experienced analysis has not been available.

PREFACE

Siblings, that magical band that is impossible to separate. From the first moment, they are bound together for the rest of their lives.

When the family increases in size and a new sibling arrives, this brings changes for all members of the family. It particularly affects our children. If they are young, they are perhaps about to enter the first crisis in their lives.

Our older daughter, Lena, was two years old when her younger brother, Ben, was born. From my studies, I was aware of the subject "dethronement trauma". Theory is very different from practice when it affects you, personally.

At the beginning with both my children, I found it to be a huge challenge. Lena found it extremely difficult to cope with the change. She showed this by pointedly provoking us and she directed her rage occasionally towards her younger brother. Sometimes we just did not know what to do. Our nights were short, our energy was at its limit and the situation was not going to improve anytime soon. We had so much hoped that our children would become inseparable.

Even though I had studied much about this subject during my training, I wanted to find out much more about it during this time. I wanted to understand why my daughter was behaving as she did. I recognised what I had not seen before and began to focus more on her needs. Indeed, the situation between the siblings really did improve. Lena seemed to understand, that her brother was not taking anything away from her and she began to feel happier and more understood. In time, her relationship towards her brother became less tense and she developed loving feelings towards him.

This made me realise how important it is to be sensitive towards your children and to try and understand what they need from us. I would like to share this experience, together with my background knowledge, with all mothers and fathers who have, or will have, more than one child.

One central aspect, which helped me immensely, was tandem breastfeeding. Because I allowed Lena to continue with breastfeeding at the same time as her brother, I had the feeling that she understood that she did not have to give up anything, but that there was enough for both of them. I am convinced that the bonds which were formed at that time strengthened their relationship.

As parents, we often do not understand why there are continual arguments. Just as I would be coming out of the children's bedroom, I could hear Lena ranting at her brother, who would promptly start to cry. I would count silently to 10 and then I would hear the cry "Mama" coming from the bedroom. It did cause us to reach the end of our patience, I admit.

You are probably thinking that they are just children and they are bound to argue. I can assure you that similar things happen in most families. Even now that my children are older, they continue to argue. That is OK and even good.

I am sure you often ask yourself why there are arguments. Why does it happen and what are the consequences? I would also like to go into this in more detail, later on. You have to look behind the façade to understand what is going on.

I am often asked how I manage to have such a harmonious family. It is not possible to explain this in a few simple sentences. It is probably a mix of the approach that my partner and I take, together with the interaction we both have with our children.

It is important for us to be empathetic and considerate with each other. Everyone has the same rights and we approach each other as equals. We consider the needs of every member of the family and orientate ourselves on the premise of so-called non-violent communication.

I would like to explain what non-violent communication is, as it is a wonderful way to communicate in an empathetic way. It has helped me on a number of occasions with conflicts and it is a way of conveying respect between the parties. I am particularly moved, when I see that my children have understood the concept, we have taught them, and sub-consciously use it.

It is particularly important to lead by example, especially when it comes to politeness. Although we do not ask our children to say "thank you", "please" or "good morning", they do it auto-matically. It is the same with apologies. We never ask for apologies, but we are very happy when one comes from the heart.

This book should help you to understand the subject of siblings better. I will give you back-ground information on which characteristics belong to which constellation of siblings and what happens with "only" children and twins. Perhaps you recognise the relationship between you and your siblings when reading this.

I would like to provide you with this guidebook, which contains tips for you and your family. As a result of my own experiences I know how difficult and challenging it can be, but at the same time, I would like to strengthen your belief that you, too, can create a harmonious family atmosphere.

This does not mean that you should not argue. That is not the aim here. My aim is to show you how you can understand each in a better way. What is going on in the heads of your children and what do they need from you?

Have patience with yourself and your children. If the situation threatens to boil over, or you are at the end of your nerves, breathe deeply. Sibling rivalry can often take us right up to the limit.

I hope I can help you, with my tips and examples from therapy and everyday life, to know that you are not alone and that there is always a way to restore family harmony.

In order to make this book easier to read, I always refer to older children in the singular, but by this I also include all other older children in the family.

The examples in this book are taken from my private life and my work experiences. All references to age are correct but I have changed the names.

- Chapter 1 -

SIBLINGS – WHAT THERE IS TO KNOW ABOUT THEM

Relationships between siblings are the longest continuous relationship in our lives. They are mostly longer than those which we have with our parents our partner, or our own children. This relationship accompanies us a whole life long. It is a link which you cannot choose but one which is given to you in life.

If you grow up with siblings, or are an only child or even with a twin at your side, this will affect you for the rest of your life.

Another form of sibling is the step-sibling. Although step-siblings are not your natural relatives, depending on how old they are when they arrive in your family and how big the age difference is, they can develop to become just as close as natural siblings are.

How have sibling relationships changed over the years? Those relationships have changed, just as our everyday life has changed. Today, most children do not grow up in large families, something which used to be more normal in previous generations. Many socio-cultural changes have occurred since then, which have reshaped the family system and its relationships.

Not only the family itself, but also its character and development depend on the sibling constellation of a family. Studies show that there are certain characteristics which can be attributed to the order of birth in the family and other constellations, although this does not necessarily have to be true of an individual case.

You will probably know the best example from your own circle of friends: There are 'only' children which are said to have the "typical" characteristic of being somewhat selfish compared to children with siblings, but then there are those, which do not fit in that description and you would think that they had grown up in a big family with lots of siblings.

This does not mean that all of the children tested in the study showed the same characteristics, but you could recognise those traits in the majority of those children.

Generally, it is interesting to see what effects the constellation of the family, or the birth order of the siblings, has on their lives and how it influences our children.

SIBLING RELATIONSHIPS IN THE PAST AND TODAY

If we look back two or three generations, we can see that children in those days grew up with many more siblings. Families were much larger and the children had little contact with the adults, compared to today. The parents went about their work and the children were often left to themselves.

The older siblings were often responsible for looking after the younger ones. Duties were clearly defined, for example the oldest sister was the head of the siblings and responsible for the work in the household.

The oldest children were an example for the younger ones. It was their duty to pass on their everyday skills to them. The younger ones were expected to obey and orientate themselves on the older ones. The aim was to be conform and uniform, adhering to tradition, morals and customs. There was little scope for individuality, no child should step out of line.

In comparison to those days, the siblings grow up very differently in our current culture. Everyday skills are most often taught by the parents to the children and there is no rank or role allocation, as was the case in the past, between the siblings. In most cases, family members are seen as equals.

In the past, individuality was an unknown concept, whereas today, families are characterised by their individuality. Siblings are encouraged to follow their own interests and give their opinions from a very young age. Individuality has become significant. Independent of class status, parenting has become more collaborative and children enjoy more equality.

An additional difference to the past is that children were not confronted with so many life changes. Today, children have to deal with many formative influences. The increase in mobility, the occupational changes of the parents, divorces, a new partner for a parent, moving home more often, changes of kindergarten / schools – these are all environmental changes which influence our children. In turn, these also effect the relationships between siblings.

Another obvious aspect is that siblings spend much less time with each other and therefore interact less. This becomes apparent, relative to the bond between them.

Siblings perform an important socialising function for each other. They can learn basic abilities, such as motoric or verbal skills from each other.

Experiences gained with our siblings during childhood can teach us how to deal with closeness, familiarity, competition and rejection, as with conflict and reconciliation.

In recent times, children spend a lot more time with their parents or other adults as previously. This leads to more pressure being brought upon the parents. Arguments used to be settled between siblings, the older ones only intervened when it was necessary but the parents were not constantly confronted with them, as they had a lot to do. That meant that conflicts between siblings used to be solved by the children themselves.

Today, the parents are the first port of call when it comes to solving conflicts between siblings. This requires much empathy and understanding on our side. We do not have to find the solutions, but we do have to guide our children, show them an empathetic way through their conflicts and support them in finding solutions.

This sounds simple but needs a lot of empathy, stamina and patience. It is always worth the effort to guide our children through conflicts. The relationship between parents and children, as well as between the siblings themselves, would be strengthened, and the basis of trust established.

SIBLING CONSTELLATIONS

You cannot influence whether you are brought up alone, with siblings or with a twin. Every form has its advantages and disadvantages. "Only" children yearn for someone to play with and the child with siblings wished he had more room or more quality time with his parents. A twin, although he has a significant bond with his sibling, perhaps wishes that he were not always considered to be one of a pair but to be recognised as a personality of his own. So, in each constellation, there are things which children cherish and things which they miss.

SIBLINGS

There is hardly a relationship in life which is so characterised by ambivalence as that between siblings. You cannot get on with them and you cannot get on without them. The relationship swings between love, familiarity, mutual support, rivalry, jealousy and hate. Nothing is left untouched.

Why is that? Research shows that siblings, which are always amicable, are suspicious. Normally, when there is an intensive and conflict-free relationship between siblings, this is a result of too little attention being paid to them by their parents. Where the parents' love is missing, siblings rely too much on each other for finding their own personal identity. A relationship between siblings, with arguments, rivalry and jealousy, is healthier than one which is always good-tempered and without strongly negative feelings.

On top, unequal treatment by the parents influences the relationship between the siblings.

If one child is favoured, this often leads to envy, jealousy and rivalry.

Research has been carried out by psychologists into the problematic aspects of sibling relation-ships, particularly with regard to sibling rivalry and jealousy.

The first fratricide in the history of mankind was said to be when Cane slew his brother, Abel, because he felt disadvantaged. There are other stories from the Bible involving Jacob and Esau, Joseph and his brothers or the lost son – all dramas of jealousy. In myths and fairy tales you find stories of one child which is disadvantaged in favour of another child. Rivalry between siblings seems to be something which has always existed.

The US American author, Francine Klagsbrun, carried out a large number of interviews with adult brothers and sisters in research for her book called "Mixed Feelings". She was most surprised by the height of emotions shown by the siblings she spoke to. Mature women suddenly spat venom and established men turned into small, insecure boys as soon as they spoke about their older brothers.

The invisible band that binds siblings is very difficult to break, even if you would like it to be cut.

There are also good sides to having siblings. They have a lot in common, especially if they are close together in years. They develop their own language and use codes to communicate. They learn to share, to take responsibility and to be caring.

With your parents, there is a dependability on them and a sense of hierarchy. This is not so with siblings, who are on an equal footing. Brothers and sisters can be gloriously direct critics. It is much easier to criticise your sibling than your parents or friends, because you do not have to expect punishment, as you do with your parents, and there are no breaks in friendship.

Sibling relationships usually undergo various phases. Although the relationship during childhood and puberty could be characterised by conflict and rivalry, siblings usually become much closer when they are adults.

"ONLY" CHILDREN

In Germany, about a quarter of all children are "only" children. Roughly half of all the children have one sibling and the other quarter are children with more than one sibling.

The cliché of the "spoilt only child" which is not able to share and is always spoilt, is one which has remained in the heads of many people. But is that really the case?

This way of thinking probably emerged in 1896 when the pedagogue, E. W. Bohannon of Clark University in Massachusetts, set a group of volunteers to fill out a questionnaire. The questions referred to the temperaments of any "only" children which the participants could think of. In nearly all cases, they were described as "excessively indulged". Other colleagues agreed with Bohannon's opinion.

In 21st century, you see the first headwind to this theory. Toni Falbo, Psychologist at the University of Texas in Austin, USA, an "only" child herself, defends herself against the notion, that only those children who have siblings can grow into respectable adults. She has worked on more than 200 studies, since 1986, and has come to the conclusion that the characteristics of children with or without siblings are no different. However, she believes that the relationship between "only" children and their parents is particularly strong.

A study, carried out in 2018 confirmed that the relationship between "only" children and their parents is perceived to be more intensive. This related particularly to the quality of the relationship between child and parent. The parent-child bond was considered to be particularly good when the child stated that he found it easy to talk to his mother and his father about important personal things.

What do "only" children say about their role? Despite close relationships with their parents, most "only" children regretted growing up without brothers and sisters. The majority missed having close playmates at their sides during their childhood.

It has been observed, that "only" children of pre-school age often create imaginative friends with whom they share their everyday lives, much more than children with siblings. It is not something which the parent needs to be worried about. On the contrary, an imaginary friend increases a child's ability to communicate and its social development. However, there are also signs that "only" children are less ready to come to agreements with others. The one-child policy in China, which has already been in place for 36 years has provided new findings on the subject. "Only" children, were said to be less good-natured. According to the "Big Five personality factors" people who are good-natured possess the following qualities: altruistic, helpful, empathetic and cooperative. Those who are not good-natured are often characterised as argumentative, mistrusting and egocentric, also showing a higher competitive spirit.

On the other hand, "only" children seemed to be more creative and better lateral thinkers. Above all, they are ahead of others when it comes to flexible thinking. One explanation could be that "only" children, which are often alone, can occupy themselves and become, of necessity, inventive at an early age.

Today, "only" children grow up differently compared to bygone days. If they have a lot of social contact, for example in kindergarten, where they are in contact with many children, the difference to those with siblings is not so great.

TWINS

There is a very striking example of identical twins: The famous "Jim twins" were identical twins which were separated from each other shortly after birth. They had not seen each other for 39 years and had no contact with each other. They took part in a twin study in Minnesota and were amazed to discover how similarly they had led their lives, even though they had been separated. Both of them had been married twice: The first time with a Linda, the second time with a Betty. They Christened their sons almost identically: "James Alan" and James Allan". Both had a dog called "Toy" in their childhood. They had also chosen similar types of work, partly in a petrol station and partly as a Sheriff's Deputy. They smoked the same brand of cigarette, both chewed their nails obsessively and in the gardens of both of them, there was a carpentered seat which circled a tree. These findings lead to the assumption that genes have an influence on our daily choices.

Twins always have a playmate of the same age at their sides, who grows up with them, is like them, who develops similarly to them and who shares their interests and passions. It seems that twins feel particularly strongly bonded with each other. In studies, the twins questioned named their most important reference person as their other twin, more than other siblings did.

Further studies revealed that twins have a very strong feeling of affinity and attachment towards each other. A comparison showed that twins were closer to each other than other siblings.

Twins rely less on their parents, friends or even partners. They find something in their relationship which other relationships cannot offer them. However, similarly to other siblings, their relationship also seems to improve over time.

Research also showed that identical twins had a stronger bond with each other than binovular twins. This is probably a result of the genetic similarity and their common experiences.

Rainer Riemann, Professor for Differential Psychology at the University of Bielefeld said that identical twins tend to have closer relationships with each other than binovular twins, who, like normal siblings only share 50% of their genetic material. This means that the genetic similarities significantly influence the quality of their relationship. He went on to say that results of studies showed that the death of one of the identical twins had a much deeper effect on the other identical twin as with the other siblings. In addition, they suffer more when they have conflicts with their counterpart. Possibly they have the thought that something must have gone terribly wrong because normally they are so similar.

Biological relationships play an important role in social relationships. People who are genetically so identical are likely to have similar perso-nalities, share similar opinions and interests, end up in similar life situations and are therefore on the same wavelength. These similarities are the basis for the relationship between identical twins.

SIBLING ORDER OF BIRTH

Recent studies show that our lives are shaped by our place in the family, whether we are born the youngest, the middle (so-called "sandwich child") or the oldest sibling. There are typical characteristics for each sibling constellation, although here you it is recognised that "exceptions confirm the rules".

In the 1920s, Alfred Adler, a development researcher, studied the question: How is it that siblings are sometimes so different? He came to the conclusion that, whether you are born as the first, middle or youngest child plays an important role on the development of a person. Adler pointed to various types of sibling who differed markedly from each other.

We remain of this opinion, even today. The psychologist and book author, Dr. Wolfgang Krüger, said that Adler was 95% correct although, in individual cases, there could be a completely different result than you would expect from the sibling constellation involved.

FIRST-BORN CHILD

The first-born child begins his life receiving the undivided attention of his parents. This gives him an advantage compared to the following children. However, the disadvantage follows very quickly: When other siblings arrive, the child has to suffer the painful experience of being de-throned. It suddenly has to share the attention with another child and must adjust to the new situation. Often, first-borns help to take care of the younger sibling(s).

This shapes their character. First-born children know that they get their attention mostly through performance. They are usually helpful and flexible, often performance-oriented and like to make decisions. They are happy to take responsibility and are regarded as reliable. You often find typical first-born children as managers or politicians. This was confirmed in a study by Rudy Andeweg and Steef van den Berger (2003), at the University of Leiden, after interviewing 1200 politicians.

According to Dr. Wolfgang Krüger, the typical characteristics of the first-born child are not only to be found in their choice of occupation, but also in private life. Many first-born children do not like to give too much of themselves and are less likely to show their affection.

THE SANDWICH CHILD

The middle child is often called the "sandwich child" because it is born between older and younger siblings.

Dr. Krüger says that sandwich children are often good at staying focused and appear to be balanced. They are happy to work behind the scenes and are ambitious, without needing to be the centre of attention.

They are good diplomats due to their role as the middle child. They are good at compromising and mediating between the other siblings. It is more difficult for a sandwich child to assert itself.

There are differences, depending on the sibling constellation in the family. If it is the only boy or the only girl among them, the situation is completely different and that child becomes the "little prince" or "little princess".

THE BABY OF THE FAMILY

The youngest child is also called the baby of the family because it receives a significant amount of attention, being the youngest and supposedly the weakest member of the family.

It distinguishes itself by its social skills and ability to get close to people. It is affectionate and devoted in personal relationships. The baby of the family likes to be spoilt in adulthood and searches for a partner who is able to take a leading position and make decisions on behalf of both of them.

The youngest ones are mostly not afraid of conflict and are independent. They prefer compromises and try to mediate in conflicts. Older siblings are more likely to be successful in performance issues whereas the baby of the family is able to be coquettish and charming.

Krüger goes on to say that the youngest are also creative and open to new things. After all, the younger sibling must find a niche for itself which is not occupied by the older siblings.

STEP-SIBLINGS

Step-siblings are not biologically related to each other but live together with one of their biological parents and the children of the step-parent in a so-called "step family".

This is not to be confused with a half-sister or half-brother, who have a common mother or father.

More and more patchwork families are popping up all over Germany and other industrial countries and logically, there are more and more step and half siblings. 850,000 boys and girls live in step-families throughout Germany, according to a study by the Federal Ministry of Family Affairs. This is probably the result of the high divorce and subsequent marriage numbers.

Researchers prefer to use a model of separating step-families according to the length of their existence. Normally, the relationship between step-siblings changes during their cohabitation in the step-family.

STEP-SIBLINGS IN YOUNGER STEP-FAMILIES

Children and youths usually arrive in a step-family after a split-up or divorce, but sometimes as a result of the death of one of the parents. Before that, they have usually lived with at least one parent (usually the mother) for a long time.

This can mean that they have a very close and high-quality relationship with that parent. Their relationship to the other parent can sometimes be ambivalent or even negative. This is often the case with the divorce of the parents, particularly when the divorce does not run amicably and there are arguments about custody and visiting rights of the children.

At the beginning, it is very difficult for children and youths of such families to integrate into, and accept, a new family. It is hard for such children and youths to accept step-siblings than it is for those who have a good relationship with both parents.

The transitional phase into the new family constellation can take many years and there is often tension and stress between the step-children.

During this period, the relationship between the step-siblings could be described as relatively cold, competitive and distant. Of course, this also depends on the age difference, the number of males and females in the family and also the behaviour of the biological and step-parents.

A too small gap between the ages of the children, children of the same gender and any authoritarian behaviour of the parents all have a negative bearing on the relationships within the step-family. In comparison, families with a larger gap between the ages of the children, children of different genders and understanding, and sensitive behaviour from the parents/step-parents, all go towards good relationships within the family.

During the first two years, the birth of a new half-sibling within the family seldom occurs, but if it happens, it can be a critical time for them, possibly effecting the relationship negatively between the step-siblings, particularly if they are young. The birth of a half-sibling causes them to lose their "baby of the family" status and there is often jealousy and negativity.

One negative aspect of there being a new sibling in a family where there are other, older children can be that the step-siblings distance themselves from the newcomer because their interests are so different and the bond is not so strong.

An average age between step-siblings of between 3 and 6 years brings clear advantages for older siblings. They can spend more time with each other, form a bond much quicker and learn to accept each other more readily.

STEP-SIBLINGS IN EXISTING STEP-FAMILIES

The relationship between step-siblings usually normalises after the initial adjustment period. However, it could take more time for each to find their role in the family. Once they have done this, the stress and conflicts usually reduce and the step-siblings start to get along better with each other.

It is much more difficult for step-siblings, who do not live in the same household but with another parent, to build up any relationship with each other. It also makes a difference whether parents or step-parents behave differently towards one or the other. If one sibling feels disadvantaged, it is likely to develop negative emotions and distance itself.

STEP-SIBLINGS IN OLDER STEP-FAMILIES

In patchwork families which have existed for five years or more, the step-children have got used to each other and build up some kind of relationship, almost like that of their biological siblings.

When the children have a smaller age gap between them, this automatically improves the intensity and closeness of their relationships, which have withstood rivalries and other difficulties along the way.

On the other hand, relationships between step-brothers and step-sisters with a large age gap of five or more years, often result in a relationship characterised by distance and rivalry.

- Chapter 2 -

SIBLING RIVALRY VERSUS FAMILY HARMONY

Families with a number of children know that it is not always harmonious. That is perfectly normal; differences of opinion, quarrels, aggressiveness and even fisticuffs between siblings is an everyday occurrence.

I know from my own experience, that it can be very stressful for a family and can test the nerves of the parents. Nevertheless, conflict has a very important role in the development and later life of the children. They can learn many basic social skills which they will need for the rest of their lives.

The harmonious family with a lot of children is, however, not an illusion. It is quite possible to aim for a harmonious family life, but first we have to understand why our children argue, then we can support them better. I will explain in the following chapter why arguments occur and how to improve the harmony in everyday family life.

COMPETITIVE THINKING BETWEEN SIBLINGS

For experiential science-based psychologists, the fight for the love of the parents is only one cause for sibling rivalry. There are other reasons, which can be stronger. It is often observed that siblings of the same gender, and with only a small age-gap between them, tend towards rivalry. This sibling constellation is like a cat and mouse game and the constant quarrels between them are a challenge for the parents and the family atmosphere.

Particularly by constant comparison between the siblings, such as "I can run quicker than you" or "My picture is much prettier than yours" leads to quarrels between them. The children compete in everything they do, because they are very similar. The genes in siblings are 50% identical and identical twins have exactly the same genetic material.

The comparisons lead to frustrations, insults and feelings of being disadvantaged. Tears flow and there is conflict. Dealing with negative feelings has to be learned and children have not yet found strategies to cope with that.

Our attitude as parents plays an important role here. If we constantly compare our children, we strengthen their competitiveness. If, in addition, one child is favoured over the other (even if only for a short time), an atmosphere of rivalry develops and with it comes feelings like jealousy and envy into their normal lives.

But it is not only the parents, who contribute to maintaining the rivalry, our community contributes too. We are judged on our performance and become rivals in the competition of recognition because of having the best performance. Life is characterised by competition and it dominates us. This is true for public areas, such as the economy, sport, politics and culture, but also in private life with regard to partnerships and family.

Children experience competition long before they reach kindergarten or school.

WHY DOES CONFLICT OCCUR? WHAT IS THE PURPOSE OF CONFLICT?

Conflict is judged negatively in our eyes. Quarrels are not pleasant. Conflict results in aggression, which can be verbal or physical. It releases negative feelings and can destroy relationships.

In reality, conflict is much more than that. Measuring up against others and making comparisons belong to the nature of mankind. Rivalry is just as much a part of humanity as friendship. Fighting and winning serves to help us survive and is part of our evolutionary roots.

Our ancestors needed to ensure their survival. Today it is not necessary to go to such lengths as to prove yourself in battle, but you can raise your position and self-esteem by winning rivalry battles. This still has meaning today, in private life, family life or within your circle of friends, but also in working life.

Particularly, children love competitions and contests. They want to measure themselves, want to win, want to be the fastest, the strongest, the best. The positive side of this is that they try to make the best of themselves.

When siblings measure themselves against each other, this results in rivalry, a competitive struggle occurs and, in the end, there are only winners. If the child wins, he can improve his self-esteem and be proud of his performance. If it loses, it has to learn to deal with frustration and disappointment.

In both cases – winner or loser – the child learns something through the rivalry. It is human nature that a child does not simply give up and step back in order to give precedence to the other child. That has to be learned.

WHAT ARE THE COMMON REASONS FOR CON-
FLICT BETWEEN SIBLINGS?

If you were to describe the reasons for conflict
from a child's point of view, the list would be
extremely long. With my children the list would
have been 1000 reasons for conflict. Even the
smallest things could lead to a quarrel. Every day
there would be new reasons for it.

Roughly summarised, the following reasons can
be given for conflict between siblings:

- The child begins to argue in order to
  release its own frustrations. There
  can be many reasons for the frustration: Stress between the parents,
  difficulties in the kindergarten,
  excessive demands at school, and so
  on. The child does not yet have a
  strategy to deal with it, so it begins to
  quarrel with its sibling as a form of
  valve.

- The child wants to draw attention to
  its needs and assert himself. Perhaps

it does not want to be disturbed during play and to build its tower in peace, without its brother or sister destroying it.

- It tries to protect the toy which is so important to it.

- The child is bored, hungry or over-tired. Its basic needs are not being met and it begins to quarrel.

The meeting of basic needs was a particularly tricky situation for us. If one or both of our children were hungry or tired, we could be sure that the next scrap was close.

They often used each other as a valve to release their emotions. When they were school age, they often argued with each other when they came home, until they had calmed down a bit.

When they were both smaller, the biggest cause of conflict was their toys. Ben always wanted what Lena had and then it went backwards and forwards. I am sure you have experienced that, have you not?

HOW CHILDREN QUARREL

In order to understand why children quarrel, it is helpful and interesting to watch their behaviour more closely.

Children have other behavioural patterns than adults when it comes to making their needs known. Adults use mostly verbal language, but particularly with small children, they do not have the language to assert themselves in words. This is why they often resort to physical means, such as hitting, biting, ripping away, pushing etc.

An example of this from my own children: Ben (2 years old at the time) wanted the digger that Lena (4 years old) was playing with. He was not able to verbalise what he wanted because he only had a small vocabulary. He ripped the digger out of Lena's hand. She did not want to give it to him so a quarrel ensued between them.

Another factor why children easily resort to physical engagement is that they have not yet learned how to control their emotions. They behave impulsively and emotionally. You could say that there is no other age when children so often display aggressive behaviour as when they are between 2 and 5. If your children are this age, you will already have felt the full force of this.

For children to behave differently during conflict, they need maturity to be able to deal with rage, aggravation or disappointment and this is a process which has to be learned. The mentoring of the parents in this respect is of utmost importance.

Conflict is all about communication. It is the most intensive opportunity to interact with one another. It does not mean that your child and its siblings do not like each other. On the contrary, the siblings sense themselves and each other much more intensively.

The children face each other closely, knowing what the other sibling likes or does not like. You often see that children "look for" conflict. They choose this way because they know well, how to acquire the attention of the other. This often happens when children are not sure how they can play together. This search for a way of interacting can be the result of the siblings having a greater difference in age or interests.

By the way, you do not only find this type of interaction between children, adults also behave similarly when they are in search of attention.

WHAT CHILDREN LEARN THROUGH CONFLICT

Conflict has positive aspects for life. Children can measure themselves with each other and learn how to protect themselves. They practise how to push through their point of view and assert themselves. It seems logical that when two siblings have differences and both try to push through their points of view and assert themselves, that this cannot take place harmoniously.

Children learn much more through conflict than we think. Conflicts teach important lessons for later life. They learn, for example:

- How to enforce their own needs
- How to define themselves
- How to respect the wishes of others
- How to deal with defeat
- How to make compromises
- How to forgive and reconcile.

APOLOGISING

On the subject of apologising, I would like to start with an example. An acquaintance of mine had twins of 3 years of age, two girls, called Leonie and Elenora. I watched the following situation play out on the playground.

Leonie took her sister's sand mould away from her. Elenora did not like that at all and through a spade at her, which hit her on the head. Leonie began to cry. The mother saw that Elenora had hurt Leonie. She said the following sentence: "Elenora, that is not nice of you. Apologise to your sister." Elenora refused to apologise, whereupon the mother repeated her demand that she should apologise. Elenora did not make any move towards obeying her mother. Only after the mother had said "If you do not apologise right now, we are going home", could you hear a quiet "sorry".

Looking at this example from the viewpoint of a three-year-old, you can see that children of that age are not yet able to feel empathy for each other. Those who do not feel empathy, do not feel guilt or remorse.

In this example, the apology did not come until the mother had made a threat, so the apology did not happen because she felt regret at what she had done.

What effect does an enforced apology have? It is possible that the negative feelings could increase. Elenora is not only enraged that her toy was taken away from her but also because she had to apologise, even though in her eyes, she had done nothing wrong. She believed only to be protecting her property. She does not yet realise that she did not choose the best way to do it. In her eyes, she has been "punished" unjustly. This can result in the child having negative feelings towards her sister and also her mother.

The mother demonstrated through forcing the apology, whom she felt was to blame. This makes her appear to show favouritism towards one party. Because of that, Elenora feels disadvantaged.

Imagine if you were to have an argument with your mother-in-law and your husband said to you: "That was not nice of you, apologise to her". How would that apology feel to you? If the apology does not come from the heart, it probably has no meaning for you. Leonie will have heard the words, but you will not really have reached her. You could say that the apology, forced this way, is superfluous and did not really have an effect.

WHAT CAN I DO?

Apologies are a form of politeness, such as "thank you", "good morning" and "goodbye".

I would like to encourage you not to force politeness or apologies onto your children. It has to come from the heart to have a meaning.

Be an example of politeness to your children. I am sure that all children will follow your lead when they are far enough in their development and it will become a matter of course for them to apologise if they see their mistakes. The apology is then meant sincerely and not because of fear of repercussions or punishment.

In the example given above, it would have been appropriate to analyse the situation and to speak to both children. Non-violent communication can help children to communicate and help them to verbalise what they wanted to express or achieve.

I will explain how non-violent communication works in the following chapter.

TIPS FOR IMPROVING FAMILY HARMONY

- Try to stay in the background and give your children space to solve the conflict by themselves. This works much better than we give our children credit for. Successfully resolving a conflict strengthens the self-confidence and lays important foundations for future conflict situations. In addition, if we intervene, we run the danger of interpreting the conflict wrongly, causing the wrong person to be punished.

- If there has already been a conflict and the resolution is not in sight, you can support them by asking: What was the reason for the argument? How did you both behave? What feelings did it provoke? Let both children explain their points of view, without interrupting them.

- Sometimes you can see an argument coming. If you see this happening, you can manoeuvre the situation in another direction, by directing their attention away from the conflict.

- Plan things with your children which they enjoy doing. For example, you can take them on an outing, to a children's party or something similar. Each child can give its input and find reasons for its ideas. Allow your children to reach an agreement on an activity.

- Let the siblings plan a project together. For example, creating a gift for an uncle or aunt, a family breakfast, making a nesting box. The children should plan together, shop together and complete the project together.

- Let the children review their day in the evenings. What did you do together? What did you enjoy about today? What did you like about each other?

- Chapter 3 -

SIBLING CRISIS INVOLVING THE FIRST-BORN

The birth of a sibling can be the first crisis in the young life of the first-born. This can be described as a dethronement trauma. Children under 3 are the most sensitive to the new situation and are the first to react to it, although it could happen with older children or possibly not happen at all. Children react in different ways; some show it by their behaviour but some reactions are more difficult to recognise.

One of the reasons why I am writing about the subject of siblings is because I realised, over the years, that a "new sibling" in the family often causes problems. Desperate mothers often ask me for advice on how to deal with the jealousy of the older child.

My experience is that parents often see that their children are suffering but do not really know how to help them. It is very important to me to be able to explain what is going on in your child's mind and how to react to it.

What I also noticed is: People recognise that there is a problem quickly when a child is seeking attention, but if that need is passive in nature, people are less likely to recognise it.

THE DETHRONEMENT TRAUMA

The arrival of a new sibling can cause the first crisis in the life of a first-born child.

They experience the arrival of the new brother or sister as being very dramatic; they are no longer the number one but have to share the attention of their parents. Particularly in the early days, when the new-born child is spending a lot of time with its mum, it is a very difficult time for the other sibling. It can cause jealousy towards the baby and it is hard for the sibling to understand why the mother is so intensively occupied with it. This can lead to behaviour, such as rejection or hostility.

Lena was 2 when her brother, Ben, was born. At first, I thought she was coping well and did not appear to be jealous. However, after the initial happiness about the baby, she became impatient, demanded my attention all the time and appeared to reject Ben.

The following example helped me to understand her better: Imagine your beloved partner suddenly brings another woman home, let's call her Beate. He pays a lot of attention to Beate and spends a lot of time with her. She is given a role in the family as a matter of course. Everyone expects you to be happy and to welcome Beate. After all, she is now a part of your family. No-one asked you if that is what you want. How would you react? Jealousy? Rage? Fear of loss? I admit, at first this example seems absurd, but for a child, it can seem exactly like that. Changes occur without consultation with it and it cannot do anything about it. The new member of the family is there and has the same rights.

We, as parents, can influence the situation. How we treat our first-born contributes greatly towards how the older children feel. When you understand the feelings which are released by the birth of a sibling, you can try to soften them and give your children support when they need it. It can help if the child receives a lot of attention from dad or another person close to it.

It does not have to result in a dethronement trauma.

Every child reacts differently and shows its feelings in its own way. It is important for us to be able to see behind the behaviour, to understand and support the child. This, in turn, serves to improve the relationships between the siblings and enhance the harmony within the family.

UNDERSTANDING DIFFERENT TYPES OF BEHAVIOUR

Each child behaves differently when faced with the arrival of a new sibling. Sometimes, this results in a physical reaction, the child itself reverts back to being a baby or it withdraws. Children are individuals and reacts in their own way to crisis-triggering situations.

Once you start to understand your child better, you can react towards it in a more understanding way. When your child feels well, you automatically feel better too.

HITTING, BITING AND FIGHTING

We often see fighting, biting and hitting in small children and it is often the reason for tears.

We adults see this behaviour negatively. You do not hit or bite. Children, particularly young ones, have not yet developed such a sophisticated language. Often, they cannot find the words they need. Hitting and biting is a form of attracting attention.

We often see and interpret prematurely. Lena blocked Ben from entering her room, by spreading her legs. "Stay out, you are not allowed in here!" or Ben suddenly screamed during play, because Lena had bitten him. Our first impulse is to say "That is not nice of you, do not be so naughty to your brother!" We are very quick to evaluate their behaviour instead of understanding why they did it.

There are many reasons why children resort to physical behaviour. This is often an impulsive reaction, because they are not yet able to think the way an adult would. Physical involvement is often a means of communication when they cannot express themselves.

Biting is a common response for children between 1 and 3. By the way, this does not always have to be for a bad reason. It could be a way of expressing positive feelings for babies on their way to becoming toddlers.

In one situation, my children were laughing and rolling on the bed together. Suddenly, Lena bit her brother. He did not understand why. Lena felt so happy and connected to her brother that she needed to give these feelings an outlet and this resulted in the bite.

It is worth looking at the situation closely. Both examples show that if a child is crying because it has been bitten, there could be a number of reasons for it.

Our children need a lot of empathy from us in understanding for what is going on in their heads. This way, we can create a trusting and strong relationship with them. However, biting and hitting should not just be accepted. I gave my children a cushion each to use, as an alternative, to release their pent-up emotions, instead of them biting their brother or sister.

REGRESSING TO BEING A BABY AGAIN

You are happy that your older child has learned to do some things independently; how to dress himself, how to eat and other such skills, because it is simpler to take care of the baby. Suddenly, the older sibling begins to behave like a baby again, sucking its thumb or speaking in baby talk.

Rebekka told me: "Marvin, my older son, was three years old when his sister, Mara, was born. At first, he seemed to be coping well with the changes in the family. I had been worried that he would be jealous after being the centre of attention for so long, but he showed interest in little Mara and did not appear to be suffering from jealousy. We were very relieved that we did not have to contend with a dethronement trauma, which a lot of people had warned us about. A few months after Mara was born, Marvin demanded that he too be fed by bottle. Up to then he had been able to dress and undress himself quite well. When I lay out his clothes, he only needed a little bit of help but he was keen to do it by himself. Now, he has started asking me to dress him. When I ask him to do it himself, he cries bitterly and becomes angry. He refuses to put his clothes on, if I do not help him. It is frustrating that he seems to be regressing in his development. I need to look after Mara and I just do not have the extra time."

Irene told me: "Anna is three and a half years old. She has been dry for about half a year. A short time ago, she got a new sister and she seemed very happy with her. What is upsetting me is that she has started to want to wear nappies once more and has become wet in the night again. I gave in to her wishes because I needed to look after the little one and did not have time to do all the extra cleaning and washing. I really hope that it is just a phase."

Usually, it is only a phase. Sometimes the older sibling does not seem to be jealous but they show us in a different way that they are missing something.

Both Marvin and Anna seem to have a loving relationship with their siblings, they are not showing any aggression or rejection towards the newborn. However, we can see from their behaviour that they needed more attention from their mum than it first appeared.

Marvin shows his needs by asking his mum to take over everyday things again for him. Anna wants to wear nappies again. In both cases, the children are demanding direct contact with their mothers.

The youngest sibling always receives a lot of attention after birth and the older child usually receives less. It sees how its mum is looking after its younger sibling, feeding it and changing its nappies. It wants to have that attention again and shows it by demanding the same.

On the other hand, it could also be a kind of copycat behaviour, to try out how it feels to have the same thing done to them. If it is only a question of trying it out, a kind of roleplay, this will get boring after a while and the child will leave the "being a baby" phase and move on to being independent again.

If the child continues to demand attention, you can help with that, using other methods. Once that the older child feels it is getting enough attention, and does not need to show the "baby behaviour", in order to get the attention it needs from mum and dad, the child's behaviour will return to normal.

This behaviour is very demanding on parents. Just at the time that the new-born needs so much care, often there is not enough time to give the other child the attention it seeks through bottle-feeding or nappy-changing. It often takes a long time before a child becomes dry and the parents are happy when it is no longer necessary. Having to change the child's nappies again leads to a great amount of frustration for the parents.

The child will continue to show this behaviour if you do not try to understand why it is happening and instead try to exert pressure to stop the behaviour. This can make the situation worse. It is more helpful to try an empathetic response, to give the child what it needs and support it.

Try allowing your child to be a baby again and respect its behaviour, even if it wants to wear nappies again or sucks its thumb. Do not worry, it will pass. When it notices that it has the same rights as its younger sibling, and it has found its place in the family again, the behaviour will subside.

Try to avoid sentences like "You are already too big for that" or "You are not a baby anymore". More sensitively, you can say "you are still my little one" because this is what your child wants you to confirm by its behaviour. Try to show it that as much as you can. It cannot slip into the role of "big brother" or "big sister" overnight and does not need to.

Something which works well against jealousy is tandem breastfeeding. This way, the child has strong proof that you are not taking anything away from it. Even if your child has passed the stage of being breastfed, it is still alright to let it try. It does not mean that it returns to breast feeding, but it does not exclude it. On the one hand it could be that your child has already lost its sucking reflex and cannot drink anymore breastmilk. On the other hand, it is possible that it no longer likes the taste. Sometimes it is better to allow the older child to try to breastfeed rather than refuse it, if the child expresses the wish to do it.

WHINING

As soon as the new-born has arrived, the older child seems to whine all the time. Everything is said in a whining, moaning tone. The child is frustrated and shows this in its language with whining.

Sometimes, it is almost impossible to bear when your child is permanently whining while you are busy with the new-born. The family harmony suffers as a result, because everyone is in a bad mood.

When the child whines, you probably tell it to speak in a normal tone when it is talking to you or you ignore the whining until it has pulled itself together and chooses a softer tone. However, it is possible that a serious crisis is bubbling up inside your child.

If your child is unable to cope with the new situation and is stressed, the whining could be a valve to show its anger. This happens sub-consciously and the child is not whining permanently on purpose. Therefore, it is not helpful for you to keep reminding your child that it needs to pull itself together. It can control itself for a short time but that does not solve its problem and the situation will not improve.

Try to put up with the whining until you have the feeling that the sibling crisis after the birth of the new-born has subsided. The situation could last from 12-15 weeks after the birth. If the older child receives enough attention from you, it will usually find its place in the family and stop whining.

It could last longer than 16 weeks, some children need more time. If the behaviour does not subside, even though you think that the new-born crisis should have passed, you can remind your child that he should speak in a more friendly way.

PROVOCATION

Provocation is one of the surest ways for children to get the attention of their parents. We always react when our children do the opposite to what we ask them.

You must not allow yourself to be provoked. The less you react to the situation, the less interesting the provocation becomes, because your child is not achieving reaction it wanted.

Your child is about to throw a glass onto the floor. Either you let him do it or you intervene, frantically. If you allow him to do it, you will notice that it was not fun for your child because you have not reacted to it. If you intervene, you give him the attention your child is seeking and it is likely to repeat the action, because it is expecting you to jump up from the sofa in order to prevent it. It is better if you divert his attention: "You have a glass in your hand, are you thirsty? Come, let us see if there is any more juice, that we can put in your glass."

It is more difficult to deal with provocations which involve the child injuring itself. For example, it bangs its head on the wall or floor or punches objects. These are extreme forms of provocation and should never be ignored.

In this situation, you should try to stay calm, but at the same time, interact with your child. The method of non-violent communication can be very useful here. An example of that is as follows: "You are so angry that you do not know how to help yourself, except by hitting that chair. I am sure it hurts. Does that help you not to feel the pain in your heart? Jealousy is really not a nice feeling. It hurts in your tummy and heart and you don't know how to deal with that horrible feeling. Come here and I will show you another way, perhaps it will help you."

At this point you can show your child alternatives, such as a pile of cushions that it can punch and let out its rage. You show that you will not accept his actions but that you understand his feelings. After a while, it will find other ways to let out its rage and the provocations will cease.

During the time that is characterised by provocation, it could happen that we misjudge an action as a provocation. Sara gives us an example out of her everyday life with 2-year-old Nora: "After the birth of her brother, Nora began to provoke me a lot. She often consciously behaved in a manner she knew I did not like. The other day, I found her with a spilt water glass and a piece of her clothing on the floor. At first, I thought she wanted to provoke me by intentionally playing with her freshly washed t-shirt in the puddle she had made. When I asked her about it, she explained that she had made the floor dirty and she wanted to clean it. Because she could not reach the cleaning cloth, she cleaned the floor with her t-shirt."

It is worth looking closely at the intentions of the child. Is it being provocative or is it doing something it is not supposed to do, unintentionally, because it did not know another way to achieve its goal? Not rushing to judgment will help you to avoid misunderstandings and to treat your child fairly. You should not just endure the provocations, but you should nevertheless show self-control and stay calm, controlling your initial impulses. Have patience with your child and it will thank you.

WITHDRAWAL

Behaviour is not always loud, noticeable or provoking. Sometimes a child will withdraw into itself, perhaps playing quietly in its room. At first, this may seem a relief for the parents, particularly when they are busy round the clock with the new-born. Parents might think that they are lucky, that the child is not jealous or has no problems with the introduction of a new sibling to the family.

Parents are mostly so busy at the beginning, that they do not notice the quiet suffering of the older child. There are also naturally quiet children, who do not suffer from the arrival of a new sibling. However, alarm bells should start ringing if a child, who normally shows a lot of emotions, such as rage or happiness, suddenly becomes quiet and withdrawn.

Other signs, that your child is suffering from stress, could be, if it suddenly begins to chew its nails, pick its nose until it bleeds or pull its hair.

All these symptoms should be taken seriously. If they are not recognised, there is the danger, that the child may develop a depression. This does not always happen, but it is important to keep this in the back of your mind in order to remain sensitive to the situation and to step in early, if needed.

I believe, that a quiet crisis of a sibling is even more challenging for the parents. Behaviour, such as provocation or tantrums, is easier to recognise and parents can react much sooner to it. Such behaviour is easier to recognise, than if a a child has needs that it cannot express, or that it is experiencing stress that it cannot handle.

You should try to find a sensitive way to approach your child. It could be a great relief for your child to be able to express its negative feelings: "I don't want my brother/sister to be here". More often, this is achieved through a third party, such as an aunt, a teacher or even a therapist. However, you can try, initially, to have that conversation with your child.

- Chapter 4 -

THE FAMILY IS CHANGING

Children in our society no longer have much to do with the subject of pregnancy, birth or baby care. During the birth, they are usually being looked after by relatives, they see their new sibling for a short time in the hospital and then later, when mum brings the little one home.

Usually, children today are not expected to have many skills in caring for a little brother or sister. In other cultures, it is normal for the other siblings to be integrated into the care of the baby and they are often allowed to carry the baby from a very early age. This is seldom the case in our society. However, if we do not allow our children to have this experience, we should not be surprised, if the contact between the siblings becomes difficult. Even older children have difficulty in understanding the needs of a baby.

The preparation for a new sibling should, in my opinion, begin during pregnancy. I think it is important to explain to older children, that there will be changes and what will be happening, then the birth will not be so unexpected. It is a good idea to prepare the older child/children what the new baby will need and what will be different. Of course, this should be explained in a positive way. I thought it was very beautiful to tell my daughter about her new brother and to introduce him, it was something we all did together.

PLANNING A FAMILY – IS THERE A PER-FECT AGE GAP?

Many parents ask themselves if there is a perfect age gap between the first and second child. Is there such a thing? Apart from the fact that nature ultimately decides that, there are certain advantages and disadvantages with each different age gap.

In addition, the priorities people set for themselves also play an important role. Would you prefer to keep the age gap as small as possible in order to return to work as soon as possible or would you rather have a greater age gap, so that you have more time with the younger one while the older one is in the kindergarten?

Even if you have already decided exactly how you would like the age gap to be, real life often chooses a different path. Did you really want to have a bigger age gap between the siblings, but you unexpectedly became pregnant? Or did you wish for a small gap between siblings, but it took longer than you wanted to become pregnant?

However it happens, each age gap, like everything in life, has its advantages and disadvantages. Sometimes you can influence the plan after which criteria are important to you and sometimes life has its own plan.

9 TO 12 MONTHS

This is the smallest possible gap. Your older child is just one year old when the sibling arrives.

Advantages:

An advantage for you is that you have the exhausting period of infancy behind you much quicker and can concentrate on other things, as they will both go into child care at about the same time.

The children practically grow up as twins because of their small age difference, they will have similar interests, it is easy for them to occupy themselves and they do not need permanent attention from you. This does not mean that there will be no conflict between them.

Disadvantages:

A new pregnancy can take a lot out of you. While you are coping with the symptoms of pregnancy, you are dealing with a new-born. The most tiring time will be at night when you will not be getting much sleep.

Your first-born is still so small that it will not understand the birth of a sibling and will need reassurance from your closeness. It is very strenuous to satisfy the needs of both babies.

12 TO 18 MONTHS

Your child is probably learning to walk when the new child is born.

Advantages:

Both children are quite close in age so that they are able to occupy themselves together, as their interests will be relatively similar.

This age gap can be an advantage for you when planning your parental leave. You can look after the children at home while they are small and when they are a little older, you can return to your working life.

Disadvantages:

The disadvantages are similar to those described above for children with an age gap of less than a year. Because their ages are close, both children will need your closeness and attention. You may also have two children at home that need their nappies changing at the same time (unless you choose to go without nappies).

2 YEARS

Many parents begin to plan for the second child when the first one is about a year old. This makes the gap between children about 2 years.

Advantages:

Many women prefer this age gap because they feel, that their bodies have recovered enough for another pregnancy.

The first child is more independent, which enables you to spend more time with your new-born.

Toys which are no longer interesting for your first child can be used by the new sibling. This also applies to clothes which your first-born has already grown out of.

Disadvantages:

The new-born will probably come during a defiant phase of your first-born, who does not particularly like what is happening. The arrival of the new baby can cause a crisis because the first-born has to share its closest caregiver.

3 YEARS AND MORE

Your child is already a little older. It is possible that it is already in kindergarten or school when its brother or sister is born.

Advantages:

With this age gap it is probable that your first-born does not feel as much jealousy or rivalry. The older sibling is already at an age, where it understands a lot more and knows its place in the family.

At this age, children often help with the care of the new-born.

Both children get their time with you. The first-born has had you to itself for three years or more. Now it is going to the kindergarten or school and therefore the new-born has more time with you alone at home.

Disadvantages:

Because the age gap is so big, the interests of the children will be different and they will probably not play together. The bond between them during childhood will not be as strong. This does not mean that it remains so in adulthood.

It could be difficult for you to get used to the sleepless nights again, after such a long time, and to start again from the beginning, just as the older child is becoming independent.

PREGNANCY

Every multiple mother can confirm that the second pregnancy is completely different from the first. With the first child you have time to lie down if tiredness suddenly takes over. You can leave the housework for a while, or the cleaning until tomorrow.

During the second pregnancy, the daily schedule is already pre-determined and does not allow as much room. "Mum, I am hungry" cannot wait until the nap time of the other child but needs immediate attention.

The morning sickness can also be very ex-hausting, if you are trying to look after a small child at the same time.

It depends on the age and development of the child as to how you speak about your pregnancy with it. Be open to all questions which your child has for you. A baby will change your routine and it is very helpful to prepare your child for the changes before the new-born arrives.

WHEN DO WE TELL OUR CHILD?

It is up to each individual, when to tell your child or children, that you are pregnant. There is no perfect time, every couple has to decide for itself when it is time to deliver the news.

If the child is still a toddler, six or seven months can seem a long time. Some parents like to tell their children immediately, others wait until the pregnancy is visible, and it could be easier for your child to understand, that a baby is growing inside its mum's tummy.

If you do not want to let others know of your pregnancy, for example within the first three months, it is advisable to wait before telling your child. You do not want your child to give the secret away to a neighbour, that mum has her baby in her tummy, news which tend to do the rounds quicker than you anticipated. On the other hand, it is good for the child to be told at the same time as others learn about it, so that it does not feel "out of the loop", which is not very nice for the child.

A lot of parents wait until after the 12th week of pregnancy to tell their child, because the time up to then is considered critical, as a lot of miscarriages happen during this time. A loss is very difficult for a child to understand. I do not mean, that you should not speak about the miscarriage at all, but that it is easier for the child to find out about it later on, when it is a bit older and can understand better what has happened. Again here, it is up to the parents to decide on the right time to discuss the subject.

Sometimes, parents have too great an expectation of their child. Particularly smaller children may not react very strongly to the news as their parents may have hoped. Please do not be disappointed about it. At the beginning your child may not be able to digest the information very well. Wait until the tummy is bigger and then the child will probably find it more interesting. Some children react more to the news and some less. Do not make it the main topic. Your child will show you when it has become interested in the baby in mum's tummy.

My rule of thumb: The younger the child, the later it needs to find out, that a new child is on the way. One-year-olds will not yet notice the growing tummy whereas a three-year-old most certainly will. Children up to the age of three years do not need much explanation. It is enough to tell them, that the baby is growing in mum's tummy.

7 TIPS DURING THE PREGNANCY

A new brother or sister will mean big changes for your first-born. You know how to avoid or reduce a dethroning trauma through good preparation. You and your partner will need to be very sensitive when dealing with the subject.

It is difficult for children to understand something, which does not affect them directly, particularly when they are younger. You can choose one of several ways to help your child to understand and include it in the process.

Here are some tips, how you can prepare your child for its new brother or sister:

1. Discovery by touch. Let your child touch your tummy. If the baby is moving, it is a good time to lay your child's hand onto your tummy, so that it can feel the movement. You can say, for example: "The baby is awake."

2. Picture books can help your child to understand the development of an unborn child. If the child is interested, it may ask questions, like how a baby is made. Here, too, I recommend you choose an age-appropriate educational book to help you explain.

3. Show your child photos and videos from the time when it was a baby itself and explain to it how it, too, once looked as a baby, giving it an idea of what to expect.

4. By use of a baby doll, which your child can care for, you can help it to prepare for the needs of your second child. For example, you can practise putting a nappy on the doll or putting a baby sling onto your child.

5. Allow your child to help with practical things, such as buying for the baby or preparing the room for the

new arrival. Perhaps your child would like to draw a picture for the baby, which it can hang in the baby's room.

6. During the pregnancy, get your child used to spending more time with the grandparents, relatives or friends, or indeed all those people who will help you once the baby arrives.

7. Stress the advantages, that living with a small brother or sister can bring: Someone your child can play with and look after, like an older person would do; to teach the baby things as it grows up, like cleaning its teeth or getting dressed.

THE BIRTH

The biggest changes start with the birth that everyone has been waiting for. But what does this mean for the older child or children? Few children are present when the baby is born. There are some women, who still give birth at home while the other children are around, but there are not many.

It is not expressly forbidden for children to go into the delivery room, but there are several reasons why this is not a good idea. Firstly, the focus is on the mother, her contractions and the imminent birth. During this time, the needs of a small child cannot be met sufficiently. In addition, it can be disturbing for a child to see its mother in such pain, particularly in the end phase where there could be screams, it could be difficult for a child to witness that.

CHILDCARE

Where should the children go during this time? Indeed, this is an increasingly difficult problem. Our social network is not as close as it once was, where we could bring the children to the neighbour at two in the morning. Often, we do not even know our neighbours and do not even say "hello" to them.

Many do not feel comfortable bringing their children to friends. Most are working people these days or have their own children and are busy enough as it is, particularly when we do not know when, and at what time, we would need their help. Even though our friends would not refuse to help, we do not want to burden them with it, just because they did not have the courage to say no.

If the grandparents live locally and we have a good relationship with them, they are often the people we call on in such situations. Perhaps we can ask a brother or sister, but mostly it is our own parents that are asked, because we know we can count on their support.

Some people do not even have that option open to them, making the question of where to bring the children a bit of a challenge. You should plan for this as soon as possible, because no one knows if the baby will come earlier than expected.

If the place is chosen early enough in advance, your child can get used to going there. It makes sense to allow your child to sleep away from home several times so that you know whether it will work well and hopefully your child will look forward to it.

If the child care is well organised, you will feel better about concentrating on the birth and the time afterwards, when you have to stay in hospital. It is a factor which is sometimes not given enough thought to, but which is of great importance.

In my experience, if the child feels happy in the care of someone who is looking after it during this time, this will set the tone for a good start with the new baby at home. It will be less stressful for you to know that your child is well looked after, because it would probably be missing the nest warmth it is used to, during that time. We want to avoid stress, in order to make the new start harmonious.

NEW SIBLING AT HOME

At last, the new baby is there and has come home. From then onwards, there will be an intensive time of changes to the new situation, which every family member will have to deal with. Take your time. It will perhaps not be smooth sailing right from the beginning, but you will find your path together.

It could be a shock for the older sibling, when mum comes home with the new baby. Here is a reminder of the example previously mentioned: Your husband brings Beate, his new wife, home with him and she is sitting quite naturally on the sofa, being hugged. As strange as that would feel to you, that is how confusing that feeling would be for your child.

It could end in a dethronement drama, because the older sibling feels neglected. Just recently, your child was being looked after by grandma and grandpa and now it wants to make up the time it missed with its mum, but she is busy with someone else. It seems that the new stranger is spending a lot of time on mum's breast.

Try to put yourself in the place of your child and understand its feelings. It will need a lot of attention and sensitivity during this time, so it can feel sure of its place in the family.

5 TIPS FOR GETTING USED TO THE TIME AT HOME AFTER THE BIRTH.

1. *Planning exclusive time:* It is very important for the older child, that it gets enough time with mum and dad or another person who means a lot to it, despite the presence of a new sibling. This means spending time with the older sibling without the baby being there. Perhaps dad could take a walk with the baby while mum plays a favourite game with the older child or reads a book with it. Be sure, that it is something that the child likes to do with its mum. I recommend planning this into your schedule as much as possible, because this helps your child tremendously to see that it is the centre of attention and the focus is not on the baby, during that time. Doing this will strengthen the parent/child relationship and also that of the child to its new sibling.

2. _Including the older child in the care of the new baby_: Even if the older sibling is still small, it can be included in everyday jobs so that the mother is not only occupied with the baby and that the child has the feeling, that it has a role in bringing up the baby. This could include small things in the care of the baby, such as fetching the nappies or spreading the baby lotion onto the tummy of the little one. It could also be fetching the baby something to wear or helping the baby at bath time. This can help to show the older child what the baby's need are, and why mum is spending so much time with it.

3. _Allow closeness_: Allow your child to cuddle its younger sibling if it wants to. Make sure, however, that the older child does not hurt the baby accidentally, because its fine motor skills are not yet fully developed.

That cuddle time will have an effect on the relationship between the siblings.

4. *Recognise needs:* Even if you have prepared your child for its younger sibling during pregnancy, that is no guarantee that it will not become jealous or aggressive of its brother or sister. The main reason for this is that the older sibling has needs which it does not feel are being met. If it begins to bite or kick, it is probably feeling neglected and wants more exclusive time with its mum or dad. It is important, that you always try to find out the reasons for this behaviour. It is not solved by saying: "Don't do that". Saying that will not change things very quickly.

5. *The role of the older siblings:* It often happens that the older sibling's new role is stressed as being "big brother" or "big sister" and with it, comes

certain expectations. Try to avoid it, if possible, because it can overstress your child and cause frustration. Although the child has become a "big brother" or "big sister" overnight, it still needs to grow into that role.

- Chapter 5 -

BREAST FEEDING – TANDEM BREASTFEEDING

Tandem breastfeeding means breastfeeding more than one child at the same time. It happens mostly by twins or triplets but it can also be a child with its younger sibling. Below I will be referring to the breastfeeding of two siblings of different ages.

For many mothers, pregnancy is the time to stop breastfeeding your first born. However, pregnant women can also breastfeed. Research shows, that tandem breastfeeding has a positive influence on the relationship between the siblings and reduces jealousy.

For those mothers who like to breastfeed for a long time, they can breastfeed, as long as it is acceptable for both mother and child or until either person no longer wishes it. Breastfeeding only works when both parties enjoy it. This also means, that if you no longer want to breastfeed your older child during your pregnancy, it is okay. You decide when the time has come for you to stop. Take no notice of the opinions of other people in this respect. The breastfeeding time is between you and your child and is an intimate form of affection towards your child. It happens, sometimes, that the child decides to stop breastfeeding during the pregnancy of its mother. The reason for that is mostly that the pregnancy happens towards the end of the breastfeeding time when the mother has little or no more milk to offer. Some children stop breastfeeding and some continue to enjoy suckling on the breast and continue to do so.

10 QUESTIONS ABOUT TANDEM BREAST-FEEDING

1. *Is it permissible to breastfeed during pregnancy?*

Yes. There is no medical reason against it, unless you are not feeling well or the breastfeeding is a burden, together with the other symptoms of pregnancy, such as nausea or tiredness.

Some women have very sensitive nipples during pregnancy. The pain can also be a reason to stop breastfeeding at that time.

2. *How does breastfeeding affect the nausea during pregnancy?*

Women usually experience less nausea while breastfeeding and there are those who feel much better doing that. There even are mothers to reach the peak of their nausea after they have given up breastfeeding. Experience shows, that breastfeeding can really alleviate pregnancy nausea, but there are few studies about it which can corroborate this.

On the other hand, breastfeeding itself can cause intense nausea with some mothers. Some notice strong feelings of nausea after commencement of milk production.

Taking care of an older child can be a hard challenge, if you are feeling queasy and tired. You should try to work on a strategy for combatting this, in order to minimise the effects. Try to maximise your intake of nutrients in your food. You may have to change your breastfeeding habits to make it more pleasant for you. Experiment with what makes you feel better. Perhaps you need to try another position or a change the frequency or length of the feed to make you feel better.

An unfavourable position during breastfeeding can cause increased nausea, particularly if the child is lying on the stomach of the mother, a position which is better to avoid, because this generally results in pressure to the stomach. Try how it feels to feed while seated or when the child lies beside you.

Some mothers are helped by a change in breastfeeding habits while others do not see a change and decide to give it up completely. Both parties should feel well during breast-feeding, so in such cases, it is better to stop breastfeeding.

3. _Does the hormone Oxytocin cause early labour?_

No. Many women are afraid that Oxytocin causes contractions, but this only occurs during the birth.

The hormone Oxytocin is also produced for other reasons, for example when you have an orgasm or during a cosy meal with friends. It is unavoidable during everyday life.

Your womb hardly reacts to Oxytocin until shortly before the contractions begin, irrespective how much of this hormone is released. This is why Syntocinon (artificial Oxytocin) does not work for pregnancy terminations.

This a reason why there are so many unsuccessful labour inductions using artificial Oxytocin. When your womb is not ready for the birth, nothing will happen, even with the hormones.

Shortly before the birth begins, the number of Oxytocin receptors in the womb increases very quickly and then the womb is ready for the function of the Oxytocin, which is to trigger the contractions. If you were to breastfeed at that moment, or have an orgasm, that could be a triggering factor to commence with the birth, but not before.

This is why the release of Oxytocin during breastfeeding is not dangerous during pregnancy.

4. *Does breastfeeding take away the nutrients needed for my unborn child?*

No. The unborn child always gets priority for what it needs. Your body takes from its reserves, if it notices a shortage of anything.

After a survey of 57 mothers, who breastfed their babies during pregnancy, all gave birth to healthy children. The average weight of those children tested was 3480g. Their weights ranged from 2530g to 4920g.

Other studies produced the result that, as long as the mother was eating enough calories in the form of a balanced diet, and as long as her weight gain was within normal boundaries, there were enough nutrients for the mother, the unborn child and the breastfeeding child. This naturally took into consideration the age of the breastfeeding child and the amount of extra food it was receiving.

5. _Does the relationship between a mother and child change while breastfeeding during pregnancy, from the mother's point of view?_

The pregnancy brings many changes with it, emotionally and physically. This can have an effect on the relationship between a mother and her child during breastfeeding. Some women are suddenly not as happy to do it as they were before the pregnancy.

Sometimes the nipples become very tender and it is painful when the child is suckling. Some women decide to stop breastfeeding, because they no longer want to or because they feel pain while doing it. Others continue. The relationship between the mother and child needs to be mutual, both participants must want to continue, so that the relationship can work.

6. *Does the breast produce Colostrum despite breastfeeding?*

Yes. The change from mature milk to Colostrum happens mostly between 4th and 8th month of pregnancy, sometimes earlier.

During birth there is a sudden reduction in Progesterone and Oestrogen concentration, which is prompted by the discharge of the placenta. The level of Colostrum increases, which releases the signal for the milk production to start. After the birth of the baby, Colostrum is only produced for a short time before the milk "comes in".

The older breastfeeding child cannot use the Colostrum. The production of milk remains intact throughout the pregnancy.

It is important to note, that when the older child takes a large amount of Colostrum before or after the birth, its bowel movements could change. Colostrum has a naturally laxative effect. This can lead to looser or more frequent bowel movements.

As soon as the milk has replaced the Colostrum, things should go back to normal.

7. _Should the first born always be fed first?_

In the first few days, until the milk production starts, it is recommended to feed the new born first. This way, the baby becomes enough "liquid gold" – the Colostrum – which is produced in the early stages. This contains important immune factors and active ingredients, which prepare the bowel of the new born for the milk which is to follow.

The Colostrum is exactly tailored to the needs of the new born and only available for a few days. Therefore, it makes sense to let the new baby feed first so that it receives all of the benefits it will need.

After the initial milk production has started, most mothers notice, that they have so much milk, that it does not matter which child goes first. By watching the behaviour of your baby, you will soon see how to deal with the situation best. Mostly, it happens on its own, without you having to think too much about it.

8. *Is there enough milk for two?*

Yes. There will be enough milk for both children. Research and independent reports show, that a mother who is breastfeeding two or more children, can produce enough milk, independent of whether they are siblings, twins or multiple births.

In a further study, it was shown, that a mother who tandem breastfeeds during the whole 7 months, during which time the older child is breastfed together with the baby, can produce double the amount of milk.

There are other factors, which can influence the amount of milk being produced, such as breast surgery, but tandem breastfeeding mothers complain more about having too much, rather than too little milk.

It is possible, that the toddler can not cope with the extra milk which is being produced after the birth and weans itself off the breast. Or perhaps it just continues and shows no signs of difficulty.

Some mothers feel it helps them, if the toddler feeds from the breast during times when engorgement or blocked milk ducts occur.

9. *What must I take into consideration regarding hygiene during tandem breastfeeding?*

Normally, there are no particular considerations when both siblings are breastfeeding. Normal bathing or showering is enough. There is no reason to clean the nipples after the feed. It is recommended not to use soap for cleansing during this time.

Even if one of the children is sick, there is no need to take special precautions. It is much more important to wash your hands more often to avoid infection, than it is to clean the nipples. The natural infection-inhibiting factors in the breast milk are enough to prevent the spread of infection.

This, however, does not apply to a yeast fungus called Candida. This is a common sickness during breastfeeding. If it has infected one person, it is important to avoid transmitting the infection from one child to another. Some sources and studies recommend that each child should have "its own nipple", during the course of the infection, and sometime thereafter.

The danger of contracting a virus, however, usually takes place a few days before the first symptoms appear, so that once the virus shows itself, it is usually too late to protect the other child. The reason for this is the proximity of the children to each other, not only during breastfeeding but also generally, around the house.

In addition, your body will already have begun to produce antibodies, which are specifically produced for that sickness, which you can pass on to your child through the breast milk. This will help the sick child to recover more quickly and at the same time prevent your other child from infection.

There are some who believe, that tandem breastfeeding even accelerates the speed of production of the antibodies. The production begins directly after the first contact with the infection.

When the older child is no longer breast-feeding and becomes sick, the antibody production does not begin until the mother or the breastfeeding baby is infected. Tandem breastfeeding would therefore become a direct method of passing on the antibodies in this case. Should you clean the nipples between feeding the siblings, it is possible that you would not only reduce the harmful pathogens, but you could also delay the production of antibodies.

10. _How does tandem breastfeeding affect sibling rivalry?_

Many mothers say that they have noticed less sibling rivalry between children who are being tandem breastfed. This is said to be the main advantage of tandem breastfeeding.

Some children like to breastfeed together. Particularly, when the older child sees the younger child being fed, it is possible that it wants to join in. You often notice that such children touch and stroke each other during the feed. It is here you can see the beginnings of the sibling bond.

Nevertheless, it is important to be aware that this is not always the case. It can cause emotional turmoil, even negative feelings between you and your breastfeeding child or between the siblings. I think it is important to have realistic expectations, because you can never predict how a situation will develop.

LONG-TERM BREASTFEEDING AND TAN-DEM BREASTFEEDING – A TABOO IN OUR SOCIETY?

"What? You are still breastfeeding?" – I am sure most long-term breastfeeding mothers have heard that more than once before. I notice that, in our society, lack of knowledge regarding breastfeeding is common and there is a lot of prejudice about it. One of the most natural things in the world is put into question, or even discouraged, suggesting that artificial milk would be better. I hear people say: "Your child is already old enough, you can change to a bottle with powdered milk" or "You will not have any more milk after such a long time, does breastfeeding still make sense?"

There is no defining moment when breastfeeding becomes long-term. It varies greatly between cultures. You could say that opinions about breastfeeding extend beyond the boundaries of the country in which you live. In Germany, the breastfeeding time is considered to be about 7.5 months. In a German study, most people stated, that breastfeeding for 15 months or more is considered unusually long.

The World Health Organisation (WHO) recommends fully breastfeeding for up to 6 months. This means, that the baby would receive only breastmilk during that time, no supplementary foodstuffs or other drinks. After the introduction of supplementary foods, breastfeeding should carry on at least to an age of 2 years because breastmilk continues to be an important source of nourishment.

The definition by the WHO shows, that long-term breastfeeding is even recommended, although it may seem somewhat strange for a lot of people.

Long-term and tandem breastfeeding mothers often have to answer a lot of uncomfortable questions and justify their actions. I often hear, that it is uncomfortable for them to breastfeed their older children in public because of the negative behaviour of other people which they have experienced.

One preconception, which you often hear, is: "Your child will never be independent, if it is always hanging on your breast and then you should not be surprised, if it gets complexes later in life."

Despite, or perhaps because of the fact, that children are breastfed for a long time, they have a good chance of growing up to be independent and self-confident. Breastfeeding is not the only aspect for good development, there are many other factors involved. Examples of such factors are: A child, that recognises its own individuality, has a healthy social environment, has loving and respectful parents and grandparents, experiences affection and a stable relationship to its mother and father.

When a mother breastfeeds her child in public, particularly one which can walk and speak, some people feel uncomfortable. In our society, the breast is not seen for its real function as a foodbank for a baby, but is primarily linked to sexual stimulation. Really, it should be easy for a mother with her experience to breastfeed long-term in public in a discreet way. You can hardly see anything of the breast and despite this, there are often discussions as to whether public breastfeeding should be tolerated or not. For me it is incomprehensible, that we have to hide our babies and toddlers when we want to satisfy their need for food, while everyone else is eating peacefully in a restaurant. Naturally, everyone has to find the way that suits them. There are no clear scientifically proven rules.

I would like to encourage you to continue in the knowledge, that long-term and tandem breast-feeding is completely natural and that you should not stop, despite what society thinks about it. The fact, is that it is best for your child and, as long as it is suitable for both of you, can only be advantageous.

- Chapter 6 -

"THAT IS MINE!" – THE PROBLEM WITH SHARING

Kerstin told a story, an example from her own experiences: "My daughter, Luana, is 2½ years old. She is quite good at amusing herself with her toys. When her brother, Lukas, 4 years old, approaches her, it often ends in conflict, because he has touched or picked up one of her toys. Luana reacts possessively and will not let Lukas play with them. For example, if Lukas picks up a cuddly toy, she starts to scream. Luana tries to take it out of his hand and if she is not successful, she will not calm down. I always try to explain to her, that she must share and that Lukas will give her the toy back soon, but she will not listen and her rage becomes worse. I am afraid, that if she does not learn it now, later she will not be able to share."

Siblings often quarrel about defending their own things. "That is mine", "No, mine", "Give it back to me" are sentences, which most parents have heard a lot.

Parents often think, that they have to teach their children early to share, otherwise they will not be able to later in life. A child of 2 years will not be able to understand that. It always ends in tears, when we take a toy away from one and give it to the other.

If our partner were to do that with our private things, such as a hairbrush, which he gives to his sister – because we can share – we are not happy, that he has done this. There are things, which belong to us, which we do not share or lend to other people. Sometimes we have to remember such examples, in order to under-stand our children better.

RECOGNISING OUR OWN SELF-AWARE-NESS

Children begin to defend their possessions at about 18 months. They do not understand, that something belongs to someone else. That recognition only comes with the milestone of seeing things in perspective. A child can only accept that another child can have possessions, when it is capable of understanding that another child may think or feel differently than it does itself.

The meaning of "mine" and "yours" is not easy for a child to understand. We are able to put ourselves in the shoes of others. This is known in psychiatry as "Theory of Mind". This ability first has to develop in children, which are very self-centred during the first three years. The child sees itself as the centre of its world and the borders to its environment are blurred. It is a process of maturity for the child to understand the feelings of others, and it happens step by step.

One way that you can see if a child has begun to understand, that there are differences between its world and those of the people around it, are tantrums. Tantrums need to be treated with a watchful eye. Tantrums are an important episode in the life of the toddler, when it learns to recognise itself as a separate entity. However, it will be years before it can understand the definition of personal property, as adults do.

You can also recognise personal identity when the child stops calling itself by name and speaks instead of "I". But remember that each child develops very differently.

WHAT HAPPENS WHEN WE FORCE OUR CHILDREN TO SHARE?

In the previous example, Kerstin tried many times, without success, to encourage her child to share. This was to be expected because, at an age of 2, children recognise their property as a part of themselves. If you try to force them to share a teddy bear or other cuddly toy, we are expecting them to give up a part of themselves. We do not really want them to do that. It will take years before they develop a sense of justice and are able to share.

It is normal, that small children do not want to or cannot share. Studies show, that children of 3 and 4 years of age hardly ever share. In 5 to 6-year-olds, the number rises to 20%. At school age, about 50% of children usually share voluntarily. This shows, that we do not have to teach our children to share, it happens automatically when they have reached a certain maturity.

WHAT CAN YOU DO?

I personally hold the view: "My child does not have to share". Other people find it difficult to understand my point of view but I stay faithful to my opinion, because it is about my child and my child's development.

We had many discussions about it within my circle of friends. Happily, I was able to placate my friends by explaining my behaviour. Some found the idea interesting and wanted to try it for themselves, others continued along their own paths, and that is also okay.

When bringing up children, it is often a question of our approach in dealing with them, or what we want to pass onto them at the end of the day.

The most important thing about sharing is, that you have to have patience with your children, as with other things. Every child develops as an individual, some quicker, some need a little longer. Pressure does not help; in fact, it causes resistance. The fact is, that they will all want to share at some time. You can support your child along the way so that it will be happy at some point in the future to share by itself, which is quite normal when it interacts with others.

RESPECTING PROPERTY

Children possess favourite things, which are important to them, just as adults do. We should respect that as parents. If they allowed to keep their own toys, and learn that their wishes are respected, they will later be able to give things up, voluntarily. Even then, they will not always want to do that. Life is a process of learning.

Again, returning to the example of Kerstin and her children: When Kerstin allows Lukas to play with the cuddly toy from Luana and tells Luana that she should share, it is almost certain to end in tears. Luana feels, that the toy has been stolen from her, because a part of her has been taken.

It would be better to respect the fact, that Luana does not want to share her toy and to explain to Lukas that the toy belongs to Luana and she does not want to share it, just as he would not like to give up his teddy. Lukas is a little older and he can perhaps understand it a bit better.

SPEAKING ABOUT FEELINGS

There is always a reason why your child does not want to give something up. It could be because it is a favourite toy, that it does not want to share. Perhaps the child is afraid that the toy will be broken or that it will not get the toy back.

It can be useful to describe the child's feelings or conflict in words: "I see Luana doesn't want to give up her toy." If possible, try not to evaluate it further.

BEING AN EXAMPLE

The most important thing about this subject is the idea of being an example. Your children learn mostly from what they see. For example, you could share your dessert with your child, offer it your drink or ask it if you can try its waffle.

The more you share things within your family, the more your child will consider it normal. Use the word "share" to describe what you are doing, so that your child understands what it means.

If you set a good example to your children, they will apply it, automatically. The gesture will come from the heart and is voluntary. That is worth so much more than when it complies to an order from the parent. The same applies to learning about politeness.

- Chapter 7 -

NON-VIOLENT
COMMUNICATION

I was looking for a simple method to help myself and others to improve communication and conflict behaviour within our family. In doing so, I came across the model of "Non-violent Communication" (NVC).

In the previous section I mentioned non-violent communication several times as an excellent way of communicating. Now I would like to explain that in more detail. This model was particularly interesting for me, because it is easy to understand and supports my principles of empathetic and need-orientated interaction. It is excellently suited for use in conflict situations between siblings but also in other situations, such as at work and in discussions with the partner, for example. We have been communicating with our partners for some time in a particular way, and our children and our children follow our example.

With this type of communication, we listen actively to each other and treat each other empathetically and with respect. We do not judge others, nor do we demonstrate power.

The non-violent communication method does not force other people to do what they do not want to do; it is a conversation at eye level and one which respects the needs of the other.

Rosenberg developed this communication concept, called "Non-violent Communication". This has nothing to do with avoiding physical violence. It is not the opposite of communicating with violence, as the name would suggest. It is much more about avoiding words of insult, intimidation or offence. This happens very often, unintentionally, in everyday life and it causes conflict.

Words like "sensitive communication", "unifying communication", "language of the heart" or "giraffe language" are often used in NVC. The giraffe is a symbolic figure for non-violent communication, because the long neck symbolises farsightedness. In addition, the giraffe has the biggest heart amongst land mammals, which symbolises compassion.

Marshall R. Rosenberg developed a concept for non-violent communication which is based on 4 steps. In the centre is empathy. I believe it would be helpful to put these four steps onto a note, which you can keep on your fridge, for example, so that you can learn them step-by-step. These steps are also helpful for your partner and older children in the family. The aim is for all members of the family to learn to communicate, non-violently with each other.

The theory is simple to understand. However, integrating it into everyday life needs a lot of practice. Your early experiences in your childhood and your habits have formed you. It will take patience to integrate a new form of communication into your family life, but it will

have an enormous effect on your understanding
of each other.

WHAT SHOULD YOU AVOID?

Avoid moral judgments if they are not necessary for your relationship; for example, if you tell your child that it is behaving badly, only because it is not doing what you want it to do in that moment. Judgment is swiftly made in sentences like "That was naughty of you", "You are impatient" or "You are so untidy". In saying these things, we are effectively ignoring the needs behind the behaviour which, in turn, prevents your child from having a sensitive interaction with you.

It is also unwise to make comparisons when talking to your child. Sentences such as "Noah doesn't cry when he has to go in the bath" or "Your sister's room always looks tidier than yours" sometimes happen unintentionally. We sometimes make comparisons of the behaviour of our children without any bad intentions. Try to focus on the child and its needs. The characters of our children are diverse, just as ours are. It is possible that a younger child does not yet clean its room, because it feels over-burdened and needs your help. Or Noah likes to go in the bath, because he is in his element there. On the other hand, little Lisa is busy with something in that moment and needs more time to find the transition to the next activity.

Something else, that I often notice, is when parents deny responsibility. "Timothy, if you have to make such a fuss, I will have to send you to your room. It is your own fault because I warned you." It is easy to deny or shift responsibility for your own decisions. Vague powers are made responsible "This is just how you do it" or "I shout at my children because I am under stress". There is also group pressure to contend with: "All my friends do it, so I do it like that" or institutional regulations, "If you do it again, you are out – those are the rules".

How can we change our communication, so that we do not morally judge, make comparisons or shy from responsibilities? The NVC method offers simple suggestions which you can use in any situation.

THE 4 STEPS

The 4 points of NVC can be noted easily on a small piece of paper, which you can hang in a place where you often go, so that you can glance at them when you pass. For you to be able to understand these points better, I have explained each of them in an example.

STEP 1: OBSERVATIONS

Describe to your child the behaviour which you have noticed and which has affected your well-being.

You should make your observation without interpreting the situation. What did you see? What happened? What did you hear? What was said? This allows your child to hear the observation without evaluation or judgment.

Why should we not judge? As soon as you do that, the probability, that your child will listen to you, reduces. Negative feelings could develop and the child feels criticised and wants to defend itself.

Instead of judging "Lisa, you are so untidy. Your things are always spread around the whole house. Tidy up immediately!" you should first describe what you have observed: "Lisa, your doll is lying under the table in the living room, your school things are spread all over the kitchen and I found your dirty clothes on the floor in the bathroom."

STEP 2: FEELINGS

Let your child know how this behaviour has made you feel.

Say what feelings you experience when observing the behaviour. How do you feel? Sad, hurt, shocked, ignored etc.

This is not really so easy. We are not used to sharing our feelings with other people. This probably dates back to our own childhoods. Our generation was brought up with the saying "keep your chin up". Feelings were not usually considered in those days. That is why it is often difficult for us to put them into words.

As an example, with Lisa: "When I see your things lying all over the place, I feel angry."

STEP 3: NEEDS

Verbalise the needs, which are behind the action.

When you explain your needs, you show, that you are responsible for your own feelings. You admit, that the trigger for your feelings is not what other people say or do, it is the present situation. It does not matter whether these are positive or negative. Feelings occur due to certain situations, such as "The house is untidy" and our need is "I expect that everyone in the family is tidy".

If you only indirectly explain your needs by interpreting and judging, you run the danger that the other person feels criticised, which in turn makes them react aggressively or try to defend themselves.

This is why it is so important to communicate your feelings and directly link them to your needs. This way, your child does not feel so offended and is more likely to react empathetically.

In our example: "When I see that the whole house is untidy, I become angry because I only feel comfortable when everything is tidy."

STEP 4: REQUESTS

Ask for a specific action. Even when this request is not complied with, that is ok.

You should formulate your request positively. This means that you should ask for a particular behaviour. If you only say what the child should not do, it knows what we do not want but not what we expect from it or what it should do. Negative formulated requests are likely to meet with defensive behaviour from your child.

This also applies to unclearly formulated requests, such as "Please pull yourself together", "be a good child" or "please be a little more friendly with each other". This only causes the child not to know exactly how it should behave.

In our example, we could speak to Lisa like this: "Could you please take your doll into your room, put your school things away and put your dirty clothes in the washing box?"

We should not use the word "please" as a demand. If the child is afraid, that a punishment may follow, if it does not follow your instructions, the request turns into a demand. This could lead to a rebellion, because it means, that your child has to subjugate itself instead of it being asked in a sensitive manner.

The more Lisa is condemned by her parents, if she does not comply with their wishes, the more the possibility that she will understand subsequent requests as demands and will react with rebellion.

Lisa does not want to comply with your request: "No, I am looking at a book with animals." We should not respond with condemnations, such as "you are lazy" or with threat of punishment: "Then I will not buy you an ice cream later" rather, we should respond to Lisa's needs in an empathetic way.

HOW CAN I REACT TO MY CHILD IN AN EMPATHETIC WAY?

Empathy means to feel how another person feels. We try to understand our child and to show it, that we understand it. We try to get rid of our pre-judgment and condemnation of our child's conduct.

We cannot solve the "problem", that the child is having at that point, but we can try to understand it and try to communicate it, using the four steps mentioned previously: Observations, Feelings, Needs, and Requests.

To be on the safe side, to ensure that we have correctly understood the principle, we can summarise the steps in our own words and repeat them. Importantly, we should put them into a question, so that we can give our child the possibility to correct the action.

This is an example of how it could look when we react empathetically towards Lisa: "Lisa, you heard my request and this has irritated you because you first want to relax after a tiring day at school. Would you like me to leave you in peace for 15 minutes?"

If Lisa feels that she is understood, it is possible that she will obey her mother's request, once she has finished what she is looking at and has calmed down. You have made a compromise. As the mother, we give our child the time it needs in that moment and, in response, the child will comply with our request. Both needs are met and both parties feel understood.

EXERCISE OF POWER

When Paul pulls his little sister's hair, you do not have time to communicate on the four-step principle. You need to act quickly and it could be useful to exercise use of power to protect Lara.

In NVC there is a difference between protective and penalising power.

Protective power means, that injury or injustice is avoided. In the above example of Paul and Lisa, you would separate Paul's fingers from Lisa's hair and separate the pair in a loving but determined way. We can use power for protective purposes, because we are directing the power towards protecting the life or rights of another, without criticising the behaviour.

Penalising power has the aim of punishing the person for breaking the rules. In an example, you would put Paul in a corner or say to him "How can you be so cruel, you should be ashamed!" If we use penalising power, we are condemning the behaviour, with the result that the child suffers for a long time, until it recognises its misdemeanour and corrects it.

In everyday life, it can be seen that punishment can lead to increasing the resistance of the child, without the child gaining insight into its behaviour.

Even if we manage to change the behaviour of the child by threatening punishment, is it not better for the child to achieve insight into its own actions?

In addition, the child would learn that the exercise of power, physically and psychologically, is socially acceptable behaviour for resolving conflicts. These are not the values that I would like to introduce to my child.

With non-violent communication, our child will not tidy its room more often or argue less with its siblings, but it can resolve conflicts and improve relationships between family members, acting as equal partners.

NVC IN EVERYDAY LIFE

Examples always make everything seem so easy. Often it is not so easy to put these into practice in everyday life. Mostly, it is ourselves who are the cause of it, often subconsciously going back to our old ways. We were brought up in a certain way and it is not easy to get rid of the old way of communication.

Using the reminder on the fridge often helped me. I needed a little time to internalise the four steps. Despite this, I often reverted back to my old communication method. If I realised at any one point, that I had done this, I thought about how I could have dealt differently with the situation, using the four steps.

It is very helpful if your partner is also included in this, so that you can help each other to recognise and implement the four steps. Speaking about this together is very useful, if there has been a conflict with the child, particularly if the third person is nearby to observe how a situation was dealt with. People who are less involved can

often see the situation with a different perspective.

I would like to emphasise how important it is to
give yourself time. Soon, you will get better at
using NVC and you will see the improvements in
your own family life.

- Chapter 8 -

IN CONCLUSION – A SUMMARY OF MY TIPS

On the following pages I have summarised the most important tips mentioned in this book. I recommend occasionally looking at the book and reading the tips, so that you can internalise them.

In addition, I am giving you some further tips on how to deal with arguing siblings, who are a bit older. This can also be useful for you in the future.

TIPS HOW TO DEAL WITH YOUR CHILD AFTER THE ARRIVAL OF A NEW SIBLING

1. *Inform the child about your pregnancy:*

When and how you tell your child is completely up to you. My tip: The younger the child is, the later I would tell it. 7 or 8 months is a very long time for young children. A one-year-old child notices changes much less than a three-year-old.

2. *Allow your child to be part of the pregnancy:*

Let your child experience the changes affecting you. Explain to it, that a little brother or sister is growing in your tummy and will soon come to live with you. Be careful, that you take its age into consideration in the explanation. Children up to three years of age do not need the explanation to be too detailed.

3. *Organise who is taking care of your child during birth and after delivery:*

Organise early where your child will be looked after during and after delivery and with whom.

4. *Protect the baby appropriately*

Avoid constant warnings like "Be careful with the baby!", "Don't hurt it!" or "Be quiet, the baby is sleeping". Your child could react defiantly, or its jealousy could increase, if it always has to take second place. Of course, you have to protect your baby, particularly when the fine motor skills of your first born are not so mature to be able to deal appropriately with the new-born. Let them cuddle. As far as loud noises are concerned, babies are really very robust and do not feel disturbed very easily.

5. *Include your child when you are taking care of your baby:*

Improve the sense of responsibility of your child by allowing it to help take care of the baby. This way it can better understand the needs of the little brother or sister and this, in turn, strengthens their relationship.

6. _Plan time to be with your older child exclusively:_

The baby will need care all day and all night. Allow your older child to be the centre of attention from time to time, because it is already used to having your attention and its needs have not changed. When Dad is at home and can look after the baby, it is a good opportunity for you to pay attention to your child. Plan something which only you two will play. You could go out for a walk or play your child's favourite game.

7. _Allow your child to be a baby again:_

Your child wants to be a baby again. Let it do that and avoid sentences like "You are already a big boy (or girl)". This behaviour does not usually last for long because it becomes too boring, as long as the baby is not taking up too much of your attention.

8.   Tolerate the whining:

Try to tolerate the whining until after the first 12 to 16 weeks and do not pay too much attention to it. It will not be long before you can mention to your child, that he should speak in a more friendly tone.

9.   Do not let yourself be provoked

Your child will provoke you. Try to stay calm to avoid encouraging your child to continue the provocation. Show your older child the boundaries during conversation. Non-violent communication can help you with this. Look beyond the behaviour to see what this provocation means, although there is not always a meaning to it.

10. Be sensitive if your child withdraws:

Be aware if your child suddenly becomes quiet and withdrawn after the birth of its younger sibling. It could be an alarm signal that it is in an after-birth sibling crisis. Help your child to verbalise its feelings, sometimes this is better with a person, who is not so close, such as a carer or someone it knows from other circles.

11. _Breastfeed both children if this is okay with you:_

Tandem breastfeeding has a very positive effect on the relationship between siblings and is very effective in avoiding or reducing jealousy. The most important thing for it to work is to ensure that both parties are happy with doing it. Listen to your inner self.

12. _Show your child alternatives to biting or hitting:_

Teach it to bite or hit into a cushion as a valve to release pent up emotions without hurting anyone.

13. _Do not force your child to share:_

Accept that your child has personal pos-sessions and avoid forcing it to share those toys with others.

14. _Speak about feelings:_

This can help to reduce the pressure from a child, particularly by jealousy. Feelings are not forbidden. Show your child that it is permitted to show negative feelings towards its baby brother or sister, and that it is quite normal.

ADDITIONAL TIPS TO USE IN CASE OF CONFLICT BETWEEN OLDER SIBLINGS

1. *Avoid punishment:*
Punishment, such as not being able to see the TV or house arrest, are more likely to cause rage and feelings of revenge.

2. *Do not step in immediately:*
Allow your children space and time to solve their own conflicts before you step in. Your children will profit from successfully solving their own conflicts. Stepping in to soon would probably have the opposite effect.

3. *Avoid comparisons:*
Try to avoid comparisons between siblings. This encourages competitive behaviour between them. It can also have the effect of forcing the child into a role, which it feels it has to continue.

4. *Do not force your child to apologise*
Allow your child time until its development has matured enough to feel empathy.

5. *Do something together:*

Regular family activities help to bring members together. Think of things which you can all do together.

6. *Allow the day to be relived together:*

Go through the day you have just experienced together with your children. Talk about what you did.

7. *Use non-violent communication:*

Try to use the rules of NVC with your children in order to resolve conflicts. Your children will learn from you and assume this form of communication with each other, automatically.

- Chapter 9 -

CONCLUSION

The subject of siblings is very complex. I was made aware of it once again while writing this book. On the one hand, we come from a family system where our role and character has been shaped, on the other hand we will establish our own family system which our children will be born into.

Naturally, the typical characteristics, which are mentioned here, relating to individual sibling constellation, are not always accurate. This is also true of only children or twins. Studies in sibling research are exciting, instructive and sometimes also useful in helping to understand certain situations. Nevertheless, I do not want to mislead you into thinking in clichés. We should always be careful in dealing with these, exceptions confirm the rules.

All the same, I think the results of these studies are exciting and I see many parallels within my family, my circle of friends and when advising other families.

The main thing I derive from those studies is, that the order in which we are born into a family, whether we are only children or twins, has an immense influence on our characters and life generally. It shapes us without us realising it.

Step-siblings also have to deal with such situations. The life that they were born into has led them into this new family system, with new step-siblings, which they first have to get to know. This is not an easy process at the beginning, until things start to settle down.

The relationship between siblings stays with them their whole life long. Even when there is a break of contact, siblings remain siblings whether there is a bond of familiarity or not. The bond is never severed.

As a child, our relationship with our siblings is different from the one we have when we are adults. I am sure that the bond between siblings begins to grow in childhood, even though it is not as strong, it is still there. Before our children become adults, we can do a lot towards strengthening or weakening those bonds.

Once again, I realised how important a harmonious family is in fostering a close sibling relationship. So if you possess the necessary background knowledge in order to prepare your older child for the changes, right from the start, when the baby starts to grow inside you, you can make it easier for your child to get used to the new baby with less jealousy and begin the relationship in a more positive way.

At the beginning it is certainly a challenge to deal with two children. Every parent has probably reached their limits in this respect. I was no different. It is extremely difficult to understand our children, if we cannot even imagine what is going on inside them.

Discussions with mothers, and the observations made within my circle of friends, have shown, that we tend to evaluate our children's behaviour very quickly without knowing exactly what caused the behaviour in the first place. It seems to be somewhere between difficult and impossible to react appropriately.

A lot can go wrong, if we interfere between siblings during a conflict. We can misunderstand the situation easily and make a wrong decision, leaving them feeling disadvantaged or not taken seriously. Feelings of being unfairly treated could then be projected onto the other sibling, which may result in feelings of revenge surfacing. I want to avoid such situations with my children and those I advise.

I have learned how important it is to be conscious of my own attitude. This is key to us dealing with our own children. I continue to follow a need-orientated approach within my family. Relationship comes before education: This is a motto that I like and which describes my attitude very well.

My form of communication – non-violent communication – is an important part of my book, as it is of my life and work. There are certainly other ways to communicate with each other in ways which achieve a harmonious family life. I have chosen this way because it is based on the needs of your child and is easy to put into practice. Of course, you need time to adapt the method into your own way of life. We have already formed our own communication patterns, which we first have to free ourselves from. If we are able to do this, we have found a wonderful way to deescalate conflict between our children. We live in the hope, that our children will automatically follow and implement this form of communication and they, in turn, will practise non-violent communication, themselves, when they interact with each other. Then they are much more likely to solve their issues among themselves without involving their parents.

I hope that my ideas and tips help you on your way towards having a harmonious family life and

I wish you strength and patience along the way. I hope that your children build a strong sibling bond and that it will become increasingly stronger throughout their lives.

DID YOU ENJOY MY BOOK?

You have read my book and know exactly what you have to do to strengthen relationships between siblings. This is why I am asking you now for a small favour. Customer reviews are an important part of every product offered by Amazon. It is the first thing that customers look at and, more often than not, is the main reason whether or not they decide to buy the product. Considering the endless number of products available at Amazon, this factor is becoming increasingly important.

If you liked my book, I would be more than grateful if you could leave your review by Amazon. How do you do that? Just click on the "Write a customer review"-button (as shown below), which you find on the Amazon product page of my book or your orders site:

Review this product

Share your thoughts with other customers

Write a customer review

Please write a short note explaining what you liked most and what you found to be most important. It will not take longer than a few minutes, promise!

Be assured, I will read every review personally. It will help me a lot to improve my books and to tailor them to your wishes.

For this I say to you:

Thank you very much!

Yours

Johanna

BOOK RECOMMENDATIONS

The Power of Breathing Techniques

Breathing Exercises for more Fitness, Health and Relaxation

We can survive for weeks without food and days without water, but only a few minutes without air.

Would it not be justified to presume that the air, which is more important for human survival than food or water, should live up to basic standards? How much air do we need for ideal breathing? And how should we breathe?

The amount of air that you breathe has the potential to change everything you believe about your body, your health and your performance.

In this book, you will discover the fundamental relationship between Oxygen and your body.

Increasing your Oxygen supply is not only healthy, it enables an increase in the intensity of your training and also reduces breathlessness. In short, you will notice an improvement in your health and more relaxation in your everyday life.

Look forward to reading a lot of background information, experience reports, step-by-step instructions and secret tips which are tailor-made to your breathing technique and help you to become fitter, healthier and more relaxed.

This book is available on Amazon!

LUTZ SCHNEIDER

LITHIUM
— AND —
LITHIUM CARBONATE

A MEDICINAL PRODUCT FOR DEPRESSION, ALZHEIMER AND DEMENTIA, FOR IMPROVING WELL-BEING AND MANAGING STRESS

100% EXPERT KNOWLEDGE

EXPERTEN GRUPPE VERLAG

MADE IN GERMANY

Lithium and Lithium Carbonate

Lithium is mostly known for its use in batteries. Most people do not realise that it is also a trace element in our bodies.

Would it not be wonderful if you could fight sicknesses, such as depression or Alzheimer, and improve your well-being, if you just had a little more Lithium in your body? What if you did not have to do anything more than take a little more Lithium?

Lithium is an important component for all of us in achieving a lasting, healthy way of life. Clinical studies and scientific articles are speaking a clear language. Despite that, Lithium is suffering a niche existence by a large majority of pharmaceutical scientists and is hardly known by the broad population. Even so, the advantages of Lithium, which lie in psychological and mental health sector, are obvious and it is easy to obtain and use.

In this book, you will discover the advantages and effects of Lithium on your body and mind.

Read about fascinating background information, scientific findings, experience reports and secret tips which are tailor-made for your needs and which will help you to achieve a healthy, longer and more fulfilling life.

This book is available on Amazon!

HOW TO BECOME
AN EARLY BIRD

The easy way to be up with the larks, using new morning routines and better sleep habits – with lots fo pratical tips

100% EXPERT KNOWLEDGE

EXPERTEN GRUPPE VERLAG

LUTZ SCHNEIDER

How to become an Early Bird

Getting up in the morning effortlessly, doing things which are good for you, things which you hardly have time for in everyday life, so that you can go to work each day with a deep inner calm. Does that sound like a perfect start to the day? Exactly! Mornings have so much more to offer than tiredness and bad moods.

Are you the type of person who would prefer to stay in bed when the alarm goes off?

Here you can learn how to change from a grumpy riser into an early bird. You will learn about your inner clock and everything you need to know about restful sleep and the various phases of sleep. You will find out about the perfect morning routine, the right nutrition and how you can activate your body and mind in the mornings. You will get step-by-step instructions how to become an early bird. That and much more is waiting for you in this book.

Read about fascinating background information, scientific findings, experience reports and secret tips which are tailor-made for your needs and which will help you to become and early bird and help you to start the day in a good way.

This book is available on Amazon!

SOURCE REFERENCES

Die Bedeutung der Geschwisterkonstellation -
Stellung in der Geschwisterreihe und deren
Auswirkungen auf das Selbstkonzept
Seminararbeit, Patrick Lustenberger, 2002

Geschwister: die längste Beziehung des Lebens
2. Aufl., von Sitzler, Susann, 2014

Geschwister
Hrsg. von Wellmann, Bettina [Hrsg.], 2012

Geschwister: Vorbilder, Rivalen, Vertraute
3. Aufl., von Kasten, Hartmut, 1999

Geschwister: Wie sie das Leben prägen
1. Aufl., von Mack, Cornelia, 2013

Geschwister chronisch kranker und behinderter
Kinder im Fokus: ein familienorientiertes
Beratungskonzept
von Möller, Birgit Gude, Marlies Herrmann,
Jessy Schepper, Florian, 2016

Geschwister: Ein Band fürs Leben.

[Schwerpunkt]

erschienen in Lernen fördern, 2009

Einzelkinder: Aufwachsen ohne Geschwister
von Kasten, Hartmut, 1995

https://www.kraftvollmama.de/gewaltfreie-kommunikation/

https://muettermagazin.com/mal-ehrlich-gibt-es-den-perfekten-altersunterscheid-zwischen-den-kindern/

https://www.spektrum.de/frage/sind-einzelkinder-anders-als-kinder-mit-geschwistern/1587834

https://www.familienhandbuch.de/familie-leben/familienformen/geschwister/geschwister rivalitaet.php

https://eltern-raten-eltern-forum.de/warum-kinder-streiten/

https://www.aptawelt.de/schwangerschaft/Zweite-Schwangerschaft/Tipps-wie-sie-geschwisterrivalitaet-vorbeugen-konnen.html

https://www.baby-und-familie.de/Erziehung/Wenn-Kinder-ein-Geschwisterchen-bekommen-102101.html

https://www.familienhandbuch.de/familie-leben/familienformen/geschwister/mitdemzweitenkindwirdallesanders.php

https://www.stillkinder.de/stillen-in-der-schwangerschaft-und-tandemstillen/

https://kellymom.com/translation-german-tandem-faq/d16milkchanges/

https://lesezeichen.rocks/uebermutter-vs-rabenmutter-chancen-und-folgen-des-langzeitstillens/

https://www.still-lexikon.de/vorteile-des-laengeren-stillens-eine-argumentationshilfe/

https://www.kinderleute.de/teilen-lernen/

https://www.leben-und-
erziehen.de/kleinkind/entwicklung-von-
kleinkindern/das-zweite-kommt

https://www.gofeminin.de/mein-
leben/geschwisterkonstellation-s2473685.html

https://www.fritzundfraenzi.ch/gesellschaft/fa
milienleben/geschwister-kriegsbeil-und-
friedenspfeife

https://www.spiegel.de/spiegel/print/d-
45280085.html

DISCLAIMER

©2020, Johanna Burgstein

1st Edition

Made in the USA
Middletown, DE
02 June 2022

66568714R00116